Hal•Leonard

Jazz Play-Along®

Book and CD for B♭, E♭, C and Bass Clef Instruments

Volume 124

Arranged and Produced by
Mark Taylor

JAZZ-ROCK
Horn Hits

10 SONGS RECORDED BY CHICAGO

ISBN 978-1-4234-9064-7

HAL•LEONARD®
CORPORATION
7777 W. BLUEMOUND RD. P.O. BOX 13819 MILWAUKEE, WI 53213

Visit Hal Leonard Online at
www.HalLeonard.com

T0088517

JAZZ-ROCK HORN HITS
10 SONGS RECORDED BY CHICAGO

Volume 124

Arranged and Produced by
Mark Taylor

Featured Players:

Graham Breedlove–Trumpet
John Desalme–Saxes
Tony Nalker–Piano
Jim Roberts–Bass
Todd Harrison–Drums

Recorded at Bias Studios, Springfield, Virginia
Bob Dawson, Engineer

HOW TO USE THE CD:

Each song has <u>two</u> tracks:

1) Split Track/Melody

Woodwind, Brass, Keyboard, and **Mallet Players** can use this track as a learning tool for melody style and inflection.

Bass Players can learn and perform with this track – remove the recorded bass track by turning down the volume on the LEFT channel.

Keyboard and **Guitar Players** can learn and perform with this track – remove the recorded piano part by turning down the volume on the RIGHT channel.

2) Full Stereo Track

Soloists or **Groups** can learn and perform with this accompaniment track with the RHYTHM SECTION only.

BABY WHAT A BIG SURPRISE

WORDS AND MUSIC BY
PETER CETERA

CD
1 : SPLIT TRACK/MELODY
2 : FULL STEREO TRACK

C VERSION

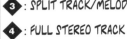

COLOUR MY WORLD

WORDS AND MUSIC BY
JAMES PANKOW

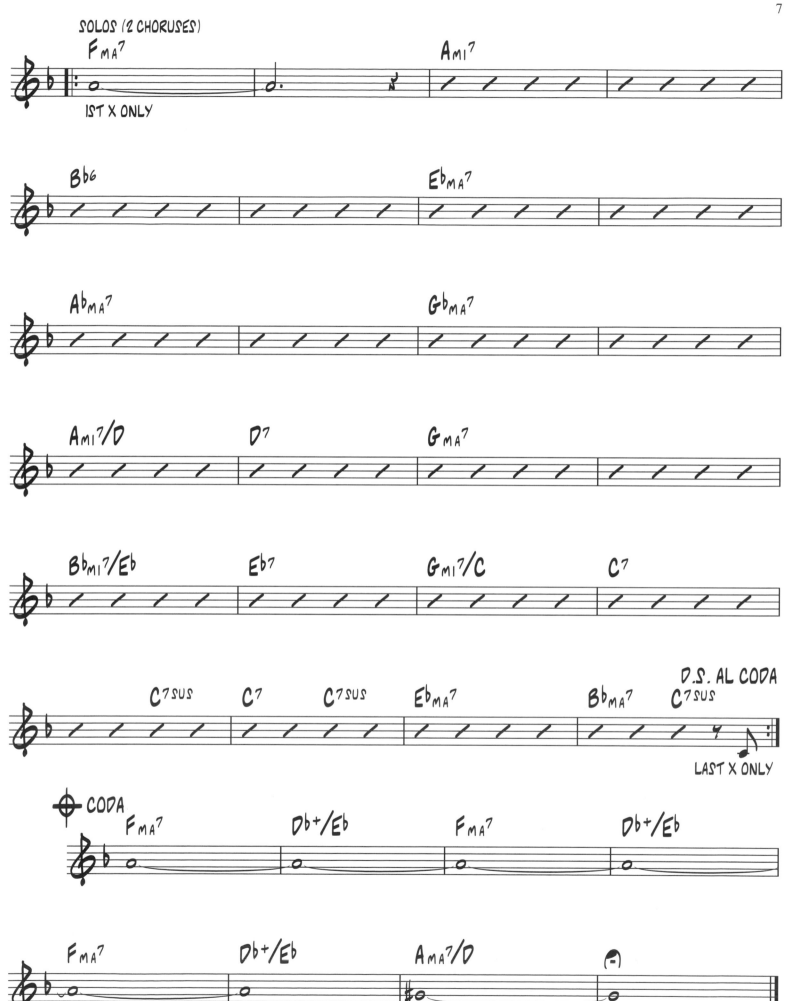

DOES ANYBODY REALLY KNOW WHAT TIME IT IS?

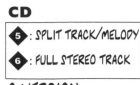

WORDS AND MUSIC BY
ROBERT LAMM

C VERSION

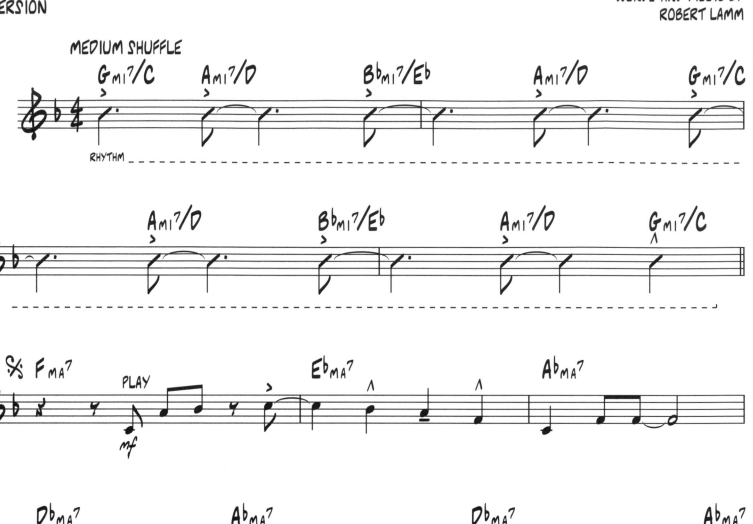

IF YOU LEAVE ME NOW

9 : SPLIT TRACK/MELODY
10 : FULL STEREO TRACK

WORDS AND MUSIC BY
PETER CETERA

C VERSION

JUST YOU 'N' ME

WORDS AND MUSIC BY
JAMES PANKOW

C VERSION

Make Me Smile

Words and Music by
James Pankow

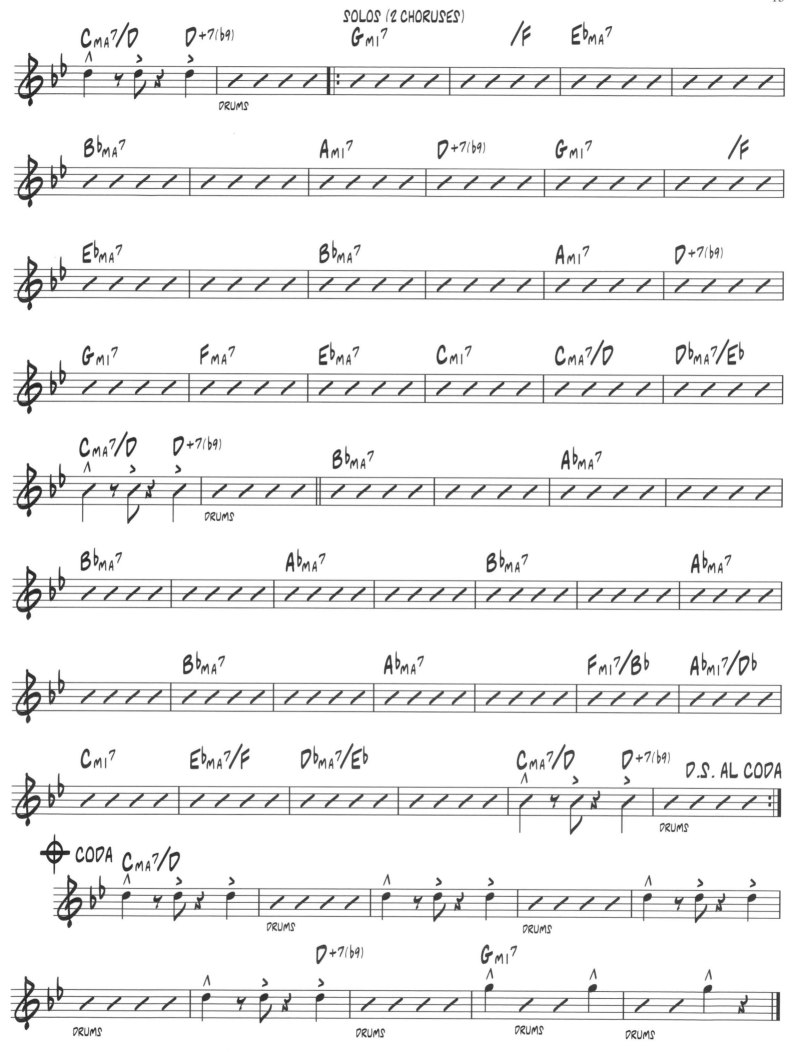

CD

15 : SPLIT TRACK/MELODY
16 : FULL STEREO TRACK

SATURDAY IN THE PARK

WORDS AND MUSIC BY
ROBERT LAMM

C VERSION

MEDIUM POP ROCK

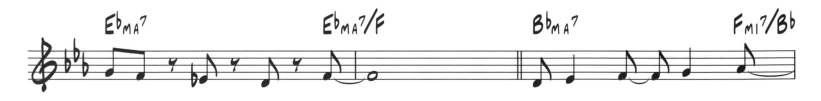

25 OR 6 TO 4

WORDS AND MUSIC BY
ROBERT LAMM

WISHING YOU WERE HERE

CD
◆19: SPLIT TRACK/MELODY
◆20: FULL STEREO TRACK

C VERSION

WORDS AND MUSIC BY
PETER CETERA

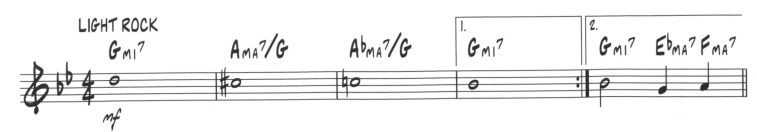

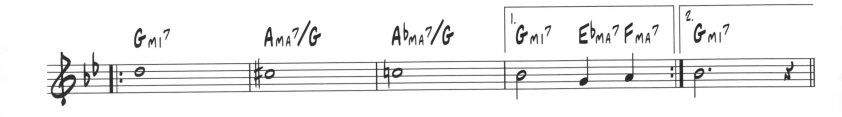

21

Hard to Say I'm Sorry

WORDS AND MUSIC BY PETER CETERA
AND DAVID FOSTER

HARD TO SAY I'M SORRY

WORDS AND MUSIC BY PETER CETERA
AND DAVID FOSTER

Bb VERSION

BABY WHAT A BIG SURPRISE

WORDS AND MUSIC BY
PETER CETERA

Bb VERSION

COLOUR MY WORLD

WORDS AND MUSIC BY
JAMES PANKOW

Bb VERSION

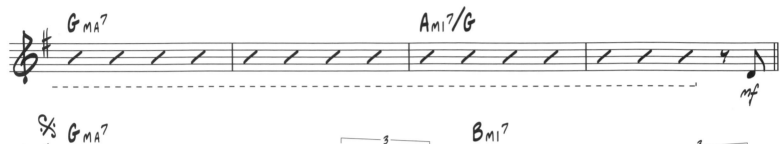

DOES ANYBODY REALLY KNOW WHAT TIME IT IS?

WORDS AND MUSIC BY
ROBERT LAMM

If You Leave Me Now

WORDS AND MUSIC BY
PETER CETERA

JUST YOU 'N' ME

WORDS AND MUSIC BY
JAMES PANKOW

MAKE ME SMILE

WORDS AND MUSIC BY
JAMES PANKOW

CD
13 : SPLIT TRACK/MELODY
14 : FULL STEREO TRACK

Bb VERSION

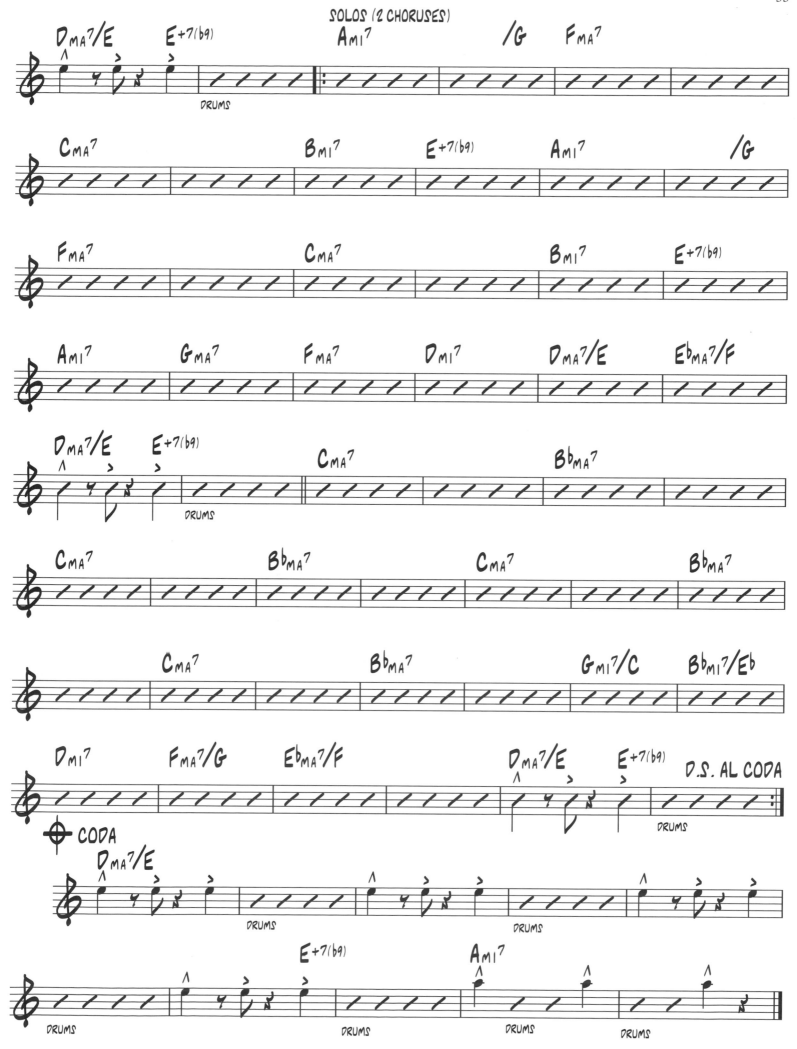

Saturday in the Park

CD
◆15: SPLIT TRACK/MELODY
◆16: FULL STEREO TRACK

WORDS AND MUSIC BY
ROBERT LAMM

Bb VERSION

MEDIUM POP ROCK

25 OR 6 TO 4

WORDS AND MUSIC BY
ROBERT LAMM

WISHING YOU WERE HERE

WORDS AND MUSIC BY
PETER CETERA

Bb VERSION

BABY WHAT A BIG SURPRISE

WORDS AND MUSIC BY
PETER CETERA

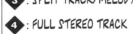
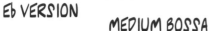

COLOUR MY WORLD

WORDS AND MUSIC BY
JAMES PANKOW

Eb VERSION

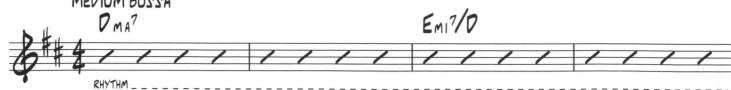

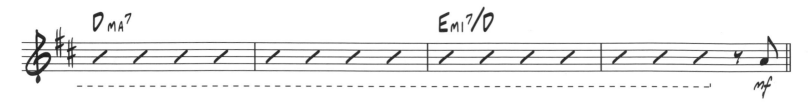

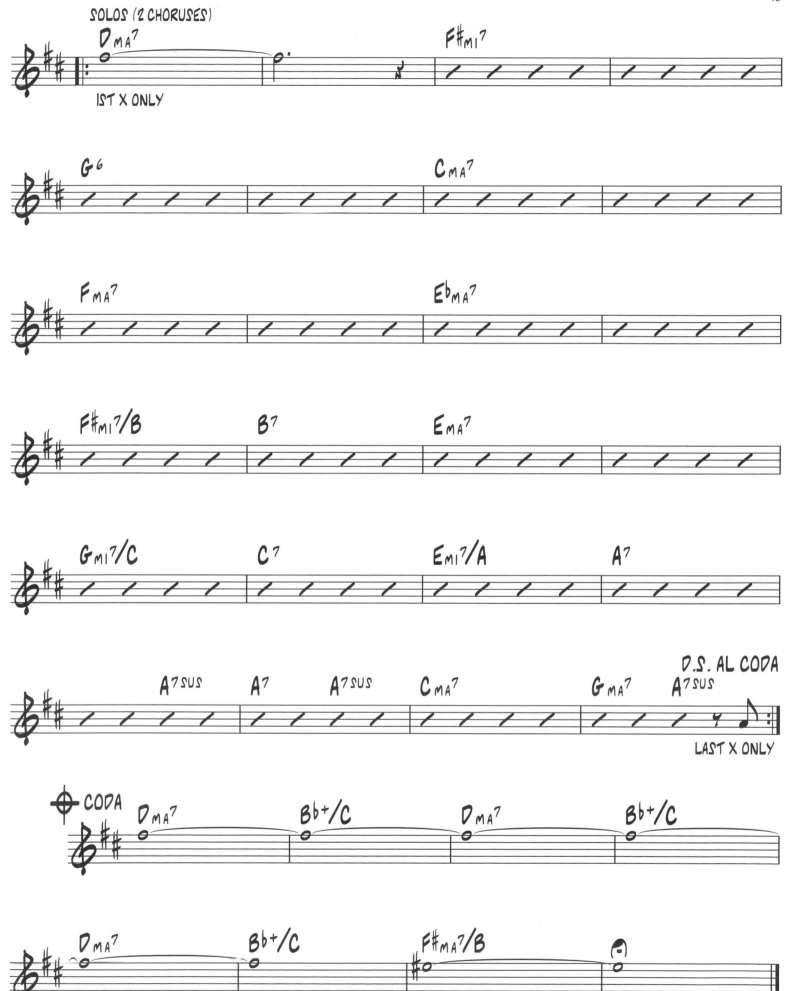

DOES ANYBODY REALLY KNOW WHAT TIME IT IS?

WORDS AND MUSIC BY
ROBERT LAMM

Eb VERSION

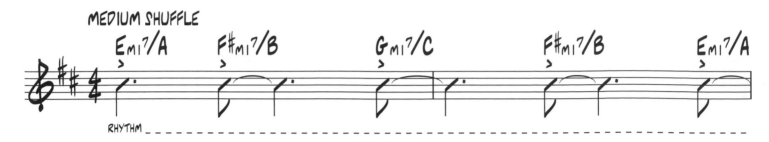

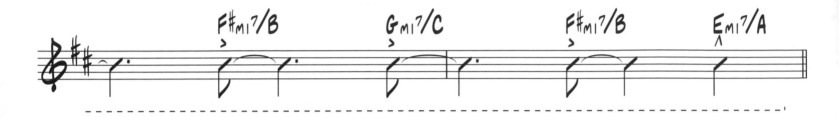

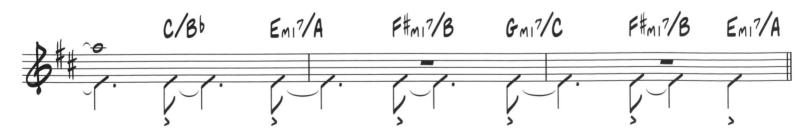

If You Leave Me Now

WORDS AND MUSIC BY
PETER CETERA

JUST YOU 'N' ME

WORDS AND MUSIC BY
JAMES PANKOW

Eb VERSION

MAKE ME SMILE

WORDS AND MUSIC BY
JAMES PANKOW

CD
13 : SPLIT TRACK/MELODY
14 : FULL STEREO TRACK

Eb VERSION

CD
15 : SPLIT TRACK/MELODY
16 : FULL STEREO TRACK

SATURDAY IN THE PARK

WORDS AND MUSIC BY
ROBERT LAMM

Eb VERSION

MEDIUM POP ROCK

25 OR 6 TO 4

WORDS AND MUSIC BY
ROBERT LAMM

WISHING YOU WERE HERE

WORDS AND MUSIC BY
PETER CETERA

HARD TO SAY I'M SORRY

WORDS AND MUSIC BY PETER CETERA
AND DAVID FOSTER

Hard to Say I'm Sorry

WORDS AND MUSIC BY PETER CETERA
AND DAVID FOSTER

BABY WHAT A BIG SURPRISE

CD

COLOUR MY WORLD

WORDS AND MUSIC BY
JAMES PANKOW

♪: C VERSION

MEDIUM BOSSA

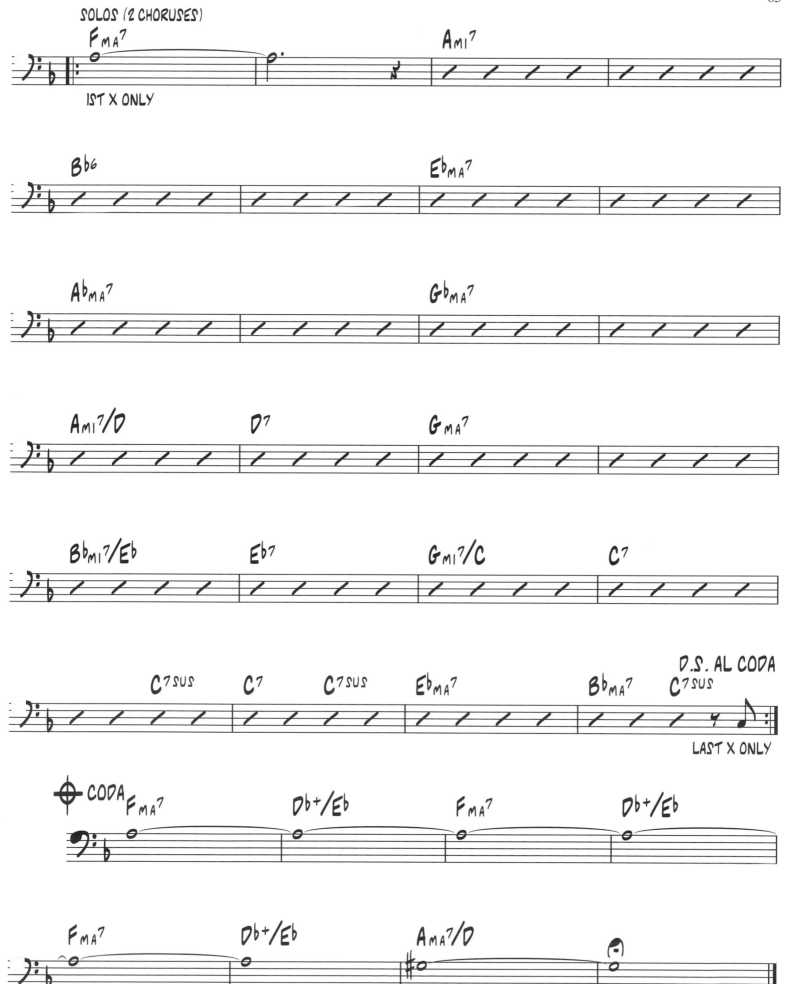

DOES ANYBODY REALLY KNOW WHAT TIME IT IS?

WORDS AND MUSIC BY
ROBERT LAMM

CD
◆5 : SPLIT TRACK/MELODY
◆6 : FULL STEREO TRACK

𝄢: C VERSION

IF YOU LEAVE ME NOW

WORDS AND MUSIC BY
PETER CETERA

JUST YOU 'N' ME

WORDS AND MUSIC BY
JAMES PANKOW

MAKE ME SMILE

WORDS AND MUSIC BY
JAMES PANKOW

♭: C VERSION

Saturday in the Park

WORDS AND MUSIC BY
ROBERT LAMM

25 OR 6 TO 4

WORDS AND MUSIC BY
ROBERT LAMM

WISHING YOU WERE HERE

WORDS AND MUSIC BY
PETER CETERA

9: C VERSION

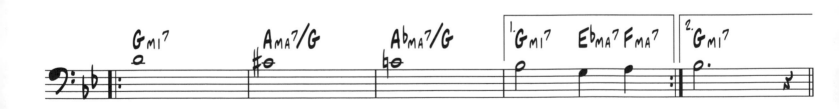

Presenting the Hal Leonard JAZZ PLAY-ALONG SERIES

1. DUKE ELLINGTON
00841644 ....$16.95

2. MILES DAVIS
00841645 ....$16.95

3. THE BLUES
00841646 ....$16.99

4. JAZZ BALLADS
00841691 ....$16.99

5. BEST OF BEBOP
00841689 ....$16.99

6. JAZZ CLASSICS WITH EASY CHANGES
00841690 ....$16.99

7. ESSENTIAL JAZZ STANDARDS
00843000 ....$16.99

8. ANTONIO CARLOS JOBIM AND THE ART OF THE BOSSA NOVA
00843001 ....$16.95

9. DIZZY GILLESPIE
00843002 ....$16.99

10. DISNEY CLASSICS
00843003 ....$16.99

11. RODGERS AND HART – FAVORITES
00843004 ....$16.99

12. ESSENTIAL JAZZ CLASSICS
00843005 ....$16.99

13. JOHN COLTRANE
00843006 ....$16.95

14. IRVING BERLIN
00843007 ....$15.99

15. RODGERS & HAMMERSTEIN
00843008 ....$15.99

16. COLE PORTER
00843009 ....$15.95

17. COUNT BASIE
00843010 ....$16.95

18. HAROLD ARLEN
00843011 ....$15.95

19. COOL JAZZ
00843012 ....$15.95

20. CHRISTMAS CAROLS
00843080 ....$14.95

21. RODGERS AND HART – CLASSICS
00843014 ....$14.95

22. WAYNE SHORTER
00843015 ....$16.95

23. LATIN JAZZ
00843016 ....$16.95

24. EARLY JAZZ STANDARDS
00843017 ....$14.95

25. CHRISTMAS JAZZ
00843018 ....$16.95

26. CHARLIE PARKER
00843019 ....$16.95

27. GREAT JAZZ STANDARDS
00843020 ....$15.99

28. BIG BAND ERA
00843021 ....$15.99

29. LENNON AND McCARTNEY
00843022 ....$16.95

30. BLUES' BEST
00843023 ....$15.99

31. JAZZ IN THREE
00843024 ....$15.99

32. BEST OF SWING
00843025 ....$15.99

33. SONNY ROLLINS
00843029 ....$15.95

34. ALL TIME STANDARDS
00843030 ....$15.99

35. BLUESY JAZZ
00843031 ....$15.99

36. HORACE SILVER
00843032 ....$16.99

37. BILL EVANS
00843033 ....$16.95

38. YULETIDE JAZZ
00843034 ....$16.95

39. "ALL THE THINGS YOU ARE" & MORE JEROME KERN SONGS
00843035 ....$15.99

40. BOSSA NOVA
00843036 ....$15.99

41. CLASSIC DUKE ELLINGTON
00843037 ....$16.99

42. GERRY MULLIGAN – FAVORITES
00843038 ....$16.99

43. GERRY MULLIGAN – CLASSICS
00843039 ....$16.95

44. OLIVER NELSON
00843040 ....$16.95

45. JAZZ AT THE MOVIES
00843041 ....$15.99

46. BROADWAY JAZZ STANDARDS
00843042 ....$15.99

47. CLASSIC JAZZ BALLADS
00843043 ....$15.99

48. BEBOP CLASSICS
00843044 ....$16.99

49. MILES DAVIS – STANDARDS
00843045 ....$16.95

50. GREAT JAZZ CLASSICS
00843046 ....$15.99

51. UP-TEMPO JAZZ
00843047 ....$15.99

52. STEVIE WONDER
00843048 ....$15.95

53. RHYTHM CHANGES
00843049 ....$15.99

54. "MOONLIGHT IN VERMONT" & OTHER GREAT STANDARDS
00843050 ....$15.99

55. BENNY GOLSON
00843052 ....$15.95

56. "GEORGIA ON MY MIND" & OTHER SONGS BY HOAGY CARMICHAEL
00843056 ....$15.99

57. VINCE GUARALDI
00843057 ....$16.99

58. MORE LENNON AND McCARTNEY
00843059 ....$15.99

59. SOUL JAZZ
00843060 ....$15.99

60. DEXTER GORDON
00843061 ....$15.95

61. MONGO SANTAMARIA
00843062 ....$15.95

62. JAZZ-ROCK FUSION
00843063 ....$14.95

63. CLASSICAL JAZZ
00843064 ....$14.95

64. TV TUNES
00843065 ....$14.95

65. SMOOTH JAZZ
00843066 ....$16.99

66. A CHARLIE BROWN CHRISTMAS
00843067 ....$16.95

67. CHICK COREA
00843068 ....$15.95

68. CHARLES MINGUS
00843069 ....$16.95

69. CLASSIC JAZZ
00843071 ....$15.99

70. THE DOORS
00843072 ....$14.95

71. COLE PORTER CLASSICS
00843073 ....$14.95

72. CLASSIC JAZZ BALLADS
00843074 ....$15.99

73. JAZZ/BLUES
00843075 ....$14.95

74. BEST JAZZ CLASSICS
00843076 ....$15.99

75. PAUL DESMOND
00843077 ....$14.95

76. BROADWAY JAZZ BALLADS
00843078 ....$15.99

77. JAZZ ON BROADWAY
00843079 ....$15.99

78. STEELY DAN
00843070 ....$14.99

79. MILES DAVIS – CLASSICS
00843081 ....$15.99

80. JIMI HENDRIX
00843083 ....$15.99

81. FRANK SINATRA – CLASSICS
00843084 ....$15.99

82. FRANK SINATRA – STANDARDS
00843085 ....$15.99

83. ANDREW LLOYD WEBBER
00843104 ....$14.95

84. BOSSA NOVA CLASSICS
00843105 ....$14.95

85. MOTOWN HITS
00843109 ....$14.95

86. BENNY GOODMAN
00843110 ....$14.95

87. DIXIELAND
00843111 ....$14.95

88. DUKE ELLINGTON FAVORITES
00843112 ....$14.95

89. IRVING BERLIN FAVORITES
00843113 ....$14.95

90. THELONIOUS MONK CLASSICS
00841262 ....$16.99

91. THELONIOUS MONK FAVORITES
00841263 ....$16.99

92. LEONARD BERNSTEIN
00450134 ....$14.99

93. DISNEY FAVORITES
00843142 ....$14.99

94. RAY
00843143 ....$14.95

95. JAZZ AT THE LOUNGE
00843144 ....$14.99

96. LATIN JAZZ STANDARDS
00843145 ....$14.99

97. MAYBE I'M AMAZED
00843148 ....$14.99

98. DAVE FRISHBERG
00843149 ....$15.99

99. SWINGING STANDARDS
00843150 ....$14.99

100. LOUIS ARMSTRONG
00740423 ....$15.99

101. BUD POWELL
00843152 ....$14.99

102. JAZZ POP
00843153 ....$14.99

103. ON GREEN DOLPHIN STREET & OTHER JAZZ CLASSICS
00843154 ....$14.99

104. ELTON JOHN
00843155 ....$14.99

105. SOULFUL JAZZ
00843151 ....$14.99

106. SLO' JAZZ
00843117 ....$14.99

107. MOTOWN CLASSICS
00843116 ....$14.99

111. COOL CHRISTMAS
00843162 ....$15.99

For use with all B-flat, E-flat, Bass Clef and C instruments, the Jazz Play-Along® Series is the ultimate learning tool for all jazz musicians. With musician-friendly lead sheets, melody cues, and other split-track choices on the included CD, these first-of-a-kind packages help you master improvisation while playing some of the greatest tunes of all time. FOR STUDY, each tune includes a split track with: melody cue with proper style and inflection • professional rhythm tracks • choruses for soloing • removable bass part • removable piano part. FOR PERFORMANCE, each tune also has: an additional full stereo accompaniment track (no melody) • additional choruses for soloing.

Prices, contents, and availability subject to change without notice.

FOR MORE INFORMATION, SEE YOUR LOCAL MUSIC DEALER, OR WRITE TO:

HAL•LEONARD® CORPORATION

7777 W. BLUEMOUND RD. P.O. BOX 13819 MILWAUKEE, WISCONSIN 53213

Visit Hal Leonard online at **www.halleonard.com** for complete songlists.

0809